HANUKKAH
The Festival of Lights

By Bonnie Bader

Illustrated by Joanie Stone

🌸 A GOLDEN BOOK • NEW YORK

Tonight we celebrate Hanukkah, the Festival of Lights.
We light the menorah.

We eat potato pancakes called latkes.

We spin the dreidel.

We celebrate Hanukkah for eight nights.
But why?

The story of Hanukkah comes from something that happened a long, long time ago to the Jewish people in the land of Israel.

King Antiochus was ruler of all the land. But he did not like the Jewish people because they did not dress, eat, or pray the same way he did.

The Jewish people prayed in the Temple. They read
from a special book called the Torah. And they celebrated
Shabbat and other holidays together in the Temple.

A beautiful menorah made of gold stood tall in the Temple. To light it, holy oil was poured into the cups. The light sparkled and glowed, filling the Temple with warmth and love.

But one day, King Antiochus announced that
the Jewish people could not celebrate their holidays,
or even read from the Torah. He ordered his
soldiers to attack the Temple.

The soldiers broke the beautiful menorah.
They even smashed the jars filled with holy oil!

Then the king's men set up statues in the Temple
so they could worship their own gods.

The Jews still studied from the Torah, but in secret. When the king's soldiers appeared, they would quickly hide the Torah and pretend they were just playing a game of dreidel!

The day came when a group of Jewish soldiers called the Maccabees decided to try to get the Temple back. They went to war against King Antiochus and his men.

But how could the small group of Maccabees defeat the king's big army?

The Maccabees did not
give up. They fought
until they won!

Then the Jewish people were able to return
to their Temple. But when they got inside, they
found a big mess waiting for them.

With the Maccabees' help, the people cleaned up and fixed the damaged Temple. And while they were cleaning, they found a small jar of holy oil.

The people built a beautiful new menorah.

When the menorah was finally lit, no one thought
the holy oil would last more than a day. To their
surprise, it lasted *eight* days. It was a miracle!

Now menorahs hold enough candles
to celebrate the Hanukkah miracle.

We light the menorah for eight days.
We remember the brave Maccabees.

We thank God for the miracle of Hanukkah as we watch the light from the candles fill our family with warmth and love.